BROADVIEW PUBLIC LIBRARY DISTRICT
2226 S. 16th AVENUE
BROADVIEW, IL 60153
(708) 345-1325

BASKETBALL LEGENDS

Kareem Abdul-Jabbar
Charles Barkley
Larry Bird
Kobe Bryant
Wilt Chamberlain
Clyde Drexler
Julius Erving
Patrick Ewing
Kevin Garnett
Anfernee Hardaway
Tim Hardaway
The Head Coaches
Grant Hill
Juwan Howard
Allen Iverson
Magic Johnson
Michael Jordan
Shawn Kemp
Jason Kidd
Reggie Miller
Alonzo Mourning
Hakeem Olajuwon
Shaquille O'Neal
Gary Payton
Scottie Pippen
David Robinson
Dennis Rodman
John Stockton
Keith Van Horn
Antoine Walker
Chris Webber

CHELSEA HOUSE PUBLISHERS

BASKETBALL LEGENDS

KEVIN GARNETT

Paul J. Deegan

Introduction by
Chuck Daly

CHELSEA HOUSE PUBLISHERS
Philadelphia

Produced by Combined Publishing, Inc.

CHELSEA HOUSE PUBLISHERS

Editor in Chief: Stephen Reginald
Managing Editor: James Gallagher
Production Manager: Pamela Loos
Art Director: Sara Davis
Director of Photography: Judy L. Hasday
Senior Production Editor: Lisa Chippendale
Publishing Coordinator: James McAvoy
Cover Design and Digital Illustration: Keith Trego

Cover Photos: AP/Wide World Photos

Copyright © 1999 by Chelsea House Publishers, a division of Main Line Book Co. All rights reserved. Printed and bound in the United States of America.

The Chelsea House World Wide Web site address is
http://www.chelseahouse.com

First Printing

1 3 5 7 9 8 6 4 2

Library of Congress Cataloging-in-Publication Data

Deegan, Paul J., 1937-
Kevin Garnett / Paul J. Deegan.
p. cm. — (Basketball legends)
Includes bibliographical references (p.) and index.
Summary: Follows the basketball career of the popular Minnesota Timberwolves forward who, in 1997, signed the largest contract in the history of pro sports.
ISBN 0-7910-5006-8 (hardcover)
1. Garnett, Kevin, 1976- . — Juvenile literature. 2. Basketball players—United States—Biography—Juvenile literature. [1. Garnett, Kevin, 1976- . 2. Basketball players. 3. Afro-Americans—Biography.] I. Title. II. Series.
GV884.G37D44 1998
796.323'092—dc21
[b] 98-46193
CIP
AC

CONTENTS

BECOMING A BASKETBALL LEGEND

Chuck Daly

What does it take to be a basketball superstar? Two of the three things it takes are easy to spot. Any great athlete must have excellent skills and tremendous dedication. The third quality needed is much harder to define, or even put in words. Others call it leadership or desire to win, but I'm not sure that explains it fully. This third quality relates to the athlete's thinking process, a certain mentality and work ethic. One can coach athletic skills, and while few superstars need outside influence to help keep them dedicated, it is possible for a coach to offer some well-timed words in order to keep that athlete fully motivated. But a coach can do no more than appeal to a player's will to win; how much that player is then capable of ensuring victory is up to his own internal workings.

In recent times, we have been fortunate to have seen some of the best to play the game. Larry Bird, Magic Johnson, and Michael Jordan had all three components of superstardom in full measure. They brought their teams to numerous championships, and made the players around them better. (They also made their coaches look smart.)

I myself coached a player who belongs in that class, Isiah Thomas, who helped lead the Detroit Pistons to consecutive NBA crowns. Isiah is not tall—he's just over six feet—but he could do whatever he wanted with the ball. And what he wanted to do most was lead and win.

All the players I mentioned above and those whom this series will chronicle are tremendously gifted athletes, but for the most part, you can't play professional basketball at all unless you have excellent skills. And few players get to stay on their team unless they are willing to dedicate themselves to improving their talents even more, learning about their opponents, and finding a way to join with their teammates and win.

It's that third element that separates the good player from the superstar, the memorable players from the legends of the game. Superstars know when to take over the game. If the situation calls for a defensive stop, the superstars stand up and do it. If the situation calls for a key pass, they make it. And if the situation calls for a big shot, they want the ball. They don't want the ball simply because of their own glory or ego. Instead they know—and their teammates know—that they are the ones who can deliver, regardless of the pressure.

The words "legend" and "superstar" are often tossed around without real meaning. Taking a hard look at some of those who truly can be classified as "legends" can provide insight into the things that brought them to that level. All of them developed their legacy over numerous seasons of play, even if certain games will always stand out in the memories of those who saw them. Those games typically featured amazing feats of all-around play. No matter how great the fans thought the superstars were, these players were capable of surprising the fans, their opponents, and occasionally even themselves. The desire to win took over, and with their dedication and athletic skills already in place, they were capable of the most astonishing achievements.

CHUCK DALY, now the head coach of the Orlando Magic, guided the Detroit Pistons to two straight NBA championships, in 1989 and 1990. He earned a gold medal as coach of the 1992 U.S. Olympic basketball team—the so-called "Dream Team"—and was inducted into the Pro Basketball Hall of Fame in 1994.

TIMBERWOLVES
21

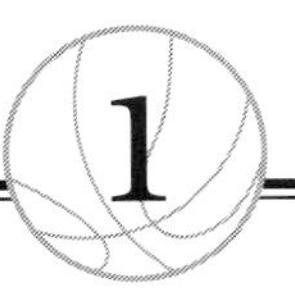

"Hitting Big Shots"

Though he had been on the floor nearly the entire basketball game, Kevin Garnett still had some energy to draw on as he fought for an offensive rebound. The 6'11", 220-pound forward grabbed the ball and slammed it through the hoop. The opposing coach, sensing Garnett's team was going to run away with the game, signaled for a timeout.

Kevin Garnett deeply wanted a victory—in fact, he felt like he had to have this game. He had been a basketball star since he was 15, but he had never played in such an important—or intense—game. It was April 28, 1998, and his team, the Minnesota Timberwolves, was seeking the second playoff win in franchise history.

The first had come only two days earlier in Seattle, where the SuperSonics and the Wolves had split the first two games of the best-of-five-games series. Everything was hanging on Game 3. A

Kevin Garnett celebrates a slam dunk in an NBA playoff game, April 28, 1998.

Minnesota victory would give the Wolves their first-ever opportunity to win a playoff series.

A screaming, sometimes deafening, capacity crowd of 19,006 fans filled the Target Center in downtown Minneapolis looking for a win. Garnett did not want to let them down.

At the Timberwolves' bench during the time-out, Garnett could barely hear Coach Phil "Flip" Saunders over the noisy crowd. As for Saunders, he was hoping a player would step up at this crucial stage of the game and lead the club to a victory.

Saunders thought Garnett might be the one to do it, especially after a play he had made on defense near the end of the third quarter. Garnett was defending against Seattle's 6'11", 250-pound forward Vin Baker, one of the best young players in the National Basketball Association.

Despite his size, Baker had very quick moves

Vin Baker of the Seattle SuperSonics dunks the ball against Timberwolves Kevin Garnett (21) and Sam Mitchell.

inside and could take a defender outside. He had given Garnett a good move right and then exploded to his left. It seemed Baker had an easy layup. Garnett, however, made a great athletic play. Unbelievably, he got a long arm up and blocked the shot, the third time he had blocked a Baker shot.

Saunders knew Garnett had the ability. With him, the underdog Timberwolves could overcome the Pacific Division champion SuperSonics, even though the odds were heavily against the Timberwolves in this Western Conference playoff series.

Seattle had reached the NBA finals two years earlier under Coach George Karl. Their 1997-98 regular season record was 61-21, third best in the league and the best in the Pacific Division. Seattle's 61 wins were 16 more than the Timberwolves recorded while finishing third in the Midwest Division. The Timberwolves were also missing two players, Tom Gugliotta and Chris Carr, both of whom had started a majority of the regular season games.

Seattle's playoff experience, their superior record, and the absence of Gugliotta and Carr from the Wolves' lineup led most to believe that Minnesota had no chance of taking the opening round series. *USA Today* predicted the SuperSonics would sweep the Wolves in three games.

Saunders, however, knew his team had already rallied from a 72-67 Seattle lead at the end of three quarters. The Wolves "small ball" attack was working. They were out-hustling the visitors even though only two reserves had seen playing time. Moving into the lead in the fourth quarter, the Wolves played impressively, often whipping the ball around until they got an open shot. As Minnesota headed back on the floor after the time-out following Garnett's slam, they held an 85-76 lead.

Garnett was playing on a rush of adrenaline, as he had been throughout the game. He had been so hyped up at the start of the game that his first shot went flying four feet over the basket. Now, he was under better control. He had shown in the past that he relished a challenge, on and off the court. Tonight, he was the player ready to step up.

He drained a 13-foot jumper. Back on defense, he snared a missed Seattle jumper and fed the ball to guard Stephon Marbury, the Timberwolves's other 21-year-old starter. Marbury buried a long three-pointer. Minnesota led 90-78 with 3:43 to play.

Forty-one seconds later, Garnett's teammates again got him the ball. On the left baseline, he was guarded by the Sonics' bulky, 6'9" forward Sam Perkins, playing in his 14th pro season. Garnett, a third-year pro, made a move on the veteran, turned, and launched a 15-footer. When the ball parted the net, the roaring crowd came to its feet. Karl put his hands over his head and pleaded for another Seattle time-out.

The Garnett basket was his seventh point in the final 5:09 of the game, and it gave the Wolves their biggest lead of the night, 93-78 with 2:59 to play. Seattle had used their third and final time-out, and Minnesota had built a lead Seattle could not overcome.

Garnett and the Timberwolves had their most impressive victory in the team's history. The final score was 98-90, and Minnesota had taken a two-to-one lead in the series.

"One more! One more! One more!" Garnett

Kevin Garnett gets high-fives from fans as they celebrate a win over Seattle in the 1998 NBA playoffs.

shouted to the crowd, stabbing the air with one index finger. Now, the Timberwolves had two chances to close out the series, one at home and, if necessary, one in Seattle.

Playing all but four minutes of the game, Garnett finished with 19 points, led the Wolves in rebounding with eight, and had six assists. On defense he had held Baker to only 17 points.

"We rode KG in the fourth quarter," Marbury said.

Garnett, meanwhile said he didn't remember his play in the fourth quarter. "I just remember the crowd going crazy. I saw opportunities to score and took them. I think [during] the first half I was a little hesitant—I don't know, just too excited. I told some of the coaches I needed to calm down, make my shots. . . ."

Minneapolis Star Tribune columnist Dan Barreiro said Garnett, "still wet behind the ears come playoff time," was marvelous, hitting big shots and grabbing big rebounds.

But perhaps Garnett's performance was not so surprising for someone who six months earlier had signed the largest contract in the history of professional sports. The first player in 20 years to jump directly from high school to the NBA, Garnett was a superstar-in-waiting. He was coming off a season in which he had broken franchise records for rebounds in a season (786) and minutes played (3,222).

He averaged 18.5 points a game, improving his scoring totals for the third time in his three-year NBA career. On March 29, 1998, he scored 32 points, his season high total. Twice before he had scored 33 points in an NBA game. He had a career high 20 rebounds against the Washington Wizards on November 13, 1997. He also set his career high assists mark during the season, getting 10 against the Denver Nuggets on January 3, 1998. In February 1998, fans had voted Garnett onto the starting five of the Western Conference team in the annual NBA All-Star Game.

"If someone had told me three years ago that Kevin would be an All-Star by now, I would have said no way," said Timberwolves vice president of basketball operations Kevin McHale at the time.

"No one thought he would succeed to the level he has as quickly as he has," said Wolves coach Saunders.

WOLVES
21

2

"I Wish I Was the Smallest Person"

Kevin Garnett was born May 19, 1976, in Mauldin, South Carolina. A suburb of Greenville, the largest city in western South Carolina, Mauldin is a middle-class town of about 12,000 residents. From sixth grade on, Kevin lived there on a street of split-level and ranch homes. One sister, Sonya, is six years older. His younger sister, Ashley, was a teenager when Garnett launched his NBA career. His mother, Shirley, married Ernest Irby, although they divorced after Kevin left Mauldin.

Kevin says his mother gave him strong values as he grew up. But she also let him make mistakes. "My mom let me mess up," he has said. His mother let him learn things on his own, helped him to understand what was happening, and gave him space.

She also taught him respect and that "to get respect, you must give it. I learned respect by watching her work her tail off to provide for us."

Kevin Garnett mugs for the camera as a Minnesota Timberwolf in his rookie year in the NBA.

Kevin's mother had never married Kevin's father, who lives in Charleston, South Carolina. Garnett is Shirley Irby's maiden name. And although Kevin's father always sent money to support him, he wasn't part of Kevin's life while he was growing up.

At the same time, Garnett did not like Ernest Irby. His stepfather never treated him like a son, which Kevin resented. When Kevin would ask for a basketball net at the house his stepfather always refused.

So Kevin played on other driveways, and, most often, at Springfield Park, a few blocks from his house. If anyone was looking for him, they knew he'd probably be at the park shooting a basketball through the chain nets. In the summers, he'd often play there from late afternoon to late at night. On Sundays, he'd run home from church, grab a sandwich, and head for the park.

Kevin's tremendous love for the game attracted notice. People in Mauldin talked about how, during basketball season, he would go straight from practice to play under the lights at Springfield Park. They knew he even played in the rain. "I don't think I ever saw a kid enjoy playing that much," said Mauldin athletic director Stan Hopkins.

Garnett attended Hillcrest Middle School, where he told everyone he wanted to be a basketball player. But he wasn't much taller than his classmates until eighth grade, and, besides, Hillcrest had no basketball team.

After middle school, Kevin decided he had to have a $100 pair of Air Jordan shoes. He saved his money and cut grass to earn more. Still, he came up short. He knew his mother didn't want to pay the difference, but he asked her anyway.

The young boy who saved for a pair of Air Jordan shoes would one day play on the same court as his hero.

She says she was in an angry mood as she drove him to the shoe store. She told him, "Boy, we gotta eat. We got bills."

Despite her displeasure, she gave him the money he needed to buy the shoes.

Years later, she recalled that on the first day of school ". . . he walked out that door and he was looking down at those shoes. He was so proud to have those shoes."

When he entered ninth grade at Mauldin High School, Kevin had grown to 6'7", much taller than his classmates. He, of course, went out for basketball. It didn't take long for Mauldin's Coach Duke Fisher to recognize Garnett's potential.

Garnett was a starter from his first game as a freshman. He displayed great defensive skills from the beginning. As a sophomore, his offense improved and he was recognized as a star player.

In years before, Mauldin High School had not been a basketball power. Soon, however, more and more people headed to the brick high school building when the Mavericks played basketball. Eventually, the team was playing to capacity crowds.

Coach Fisher would later say Garnett was "the best player I ever saw, and I've been coaching 25 years. He can do everything on a basketball court. You dream of coaching a player like that sometime in your career, and you don't think it will ever come."

By the end of Garnett's sophomore year in high school, he was attracting national attention. That summer, he was ranked the No. 1 player in the Nike All-American Basketball Festival in Indianapolis, Indiana.

Meanwhile, Kevin's mother was thinking about taking her son out of the spotlight in Mauldin. Kevin had become so well-known in town that almost everyone recognized him. In Mauldin, he could no longer be a normal kid.

And he did not like the spotlight. "I just want to be like everyone else," he once told a friend who had coached him in off-season basketball tournaments.

"I'll never forget him telling me, 'Coach, sometimes I wish I was the smallest person at school.

This is too much,'" said one of his high school coaches.

Shirley Irby thought Kevin might do better in the classroom if he were somewhere else. In the summer of 1993, Kevin and his mother visited a school in Virginia. Oak Hill Academy in Mouth of Wilson, Virginia, brings in high school players from many states and plays a national schedule. Oak Hill wanted Kevin, but his mother was not impressed.

Kevin returned to Mauldin High School for his junior year as college recruiters pegged him as the top prospect in the United States. He struggled to cope with the growing attention his basketball skills were attracting, and his classroom work suffered. Teachers at Mauldin believed he was bright and capable of doing well in all subjects. However, they saw him doing poorly in English and Spanish, although he was doing fine in math and history.

Kevin's history teacher during his junior year befriended him. He called Janie Willoughby "Mama Will." She realized that all the attention Kevin was receiving sometimes made it difficult for him to stay focused in the classroom. He appreciated her attention and got a B in her class.

The many distractions for the teenage basketball star included recruiting letters from colleges. Garnett received so many letters that he sometimes had teachers and other students open some of them.

On the basketball floor, Kevin was now a 6'9" powerhouse. "The kid can do things with the basketball," Coach Fisher said. "He's got great hands, great feet. He can put it on the floor like a guard.

"We kept him inside. But if he wanted to shoot the 15-footer, that was fine, 'cause he had great touch. And he was the most unselfish good player I ever saw."

In March 1994, Garnett led the Mavericks to the South Carolina Class AAAA tournament semifinals. In a quarterfinal game, Garnett scored 37 points and had 24 rebounds and six blocks in a 60-55 win over the Lexington Wildcats.

But the season ended four days later when 3,500 fans watched the Dormam Cavaliers defeat the Mavericks, 70-58. After the season, Garnett was named a first-team Parade All-American.

Kevin might have stayed in Mauldin to grad-

Now an NBA star, Kevin returns to his old school in South Carolina to encourage young children with basketball dreams.

uate, but in May 1994 he and four other students were involved in a fracas at school. All five were arrested. Eventually, they were put through a pretrial program for first offenders and the charges were dropped. Even so, it was unclear whether Garnett would be allowed to return to Mauldin High School in the fall of 1994. That made the decision to go elsewhere a fairly easy one.

34

3

ON TO THE BIG CITY

Elsewhere turned out to be Chicago. The 18-year-old kid left his hometown in the quiet South Carolina countryside before his senior year to travel almost 800 miles to the busy streets of one of the nation's largest cities.

The decision to move to Chicago came after Garnett and his mother went to a Nike basketball camp in suburban Chicago in July 1994. Farragut Academy coach William "Wolf" Nelson was one of the camp's coaches. Ronnie Fields, a Farragut star player, was also at the camp, and Garnett knew Fields from attending a Nike event the year before.

Garnett knew that if he played basketball in Chicago he would not be the focus of the entire city. The idea of going up against the excellent players in the Chicago public league also appealed to him. So did the chance to play with Fields.

So, in August 1994, Garnett went to the big

Kevin transferred to Farragut Academy in his senior year of high school.

city. He, his mother, and Ashley moved into an apartment in the gang-ridden west side of Chicago. Their apartment was one floor above Coach Nelson's.

A friend from childhood, Jamie Peters, also enrolled at Farragut. He was unhappy in Chicago, however, and soon returned to South Carolina.

Garnett stayed.

Garnett enjoyed playing for his second high school team, the Farragut Academy Admirals.

"This is the first time I've been able to relax and concentrate on what I have to do," said Garnett. In Chicago, he was "not the only focus for the people and the media. I'm just one fish in the ocean."

Garnett enrolled at Farragut Academy, a public school. The student body had changed from mostly white in the 1960s to mostly black in the 1970s to mostly Hispanic when Kevin arrived. There were more than 2,000 students, but there were only 287 seniors compared to more than 1,000 freshmen, reflecting a huge dropout rate.

The school's dress code called for black pants and white T-shirts for boys. Among the things forbidden by a strict discipline policy were gang signals. Police officers were at each of the four corners of the Farragut block when school was dismissed each day.

Garnett later said he toughened up in the year he spent at Farragut. "I got a lot of what you call 'dog' and an aggressive attitude toward the game. To be able to rebound or dunk with a snarl face,

I think it went to another level once I played in Chicago. You've got to be strong."

Meanwhile, Coach Nelson, who had grown up in Chicago's inner-city neighborhoods, found he had a team with a wealth of talent when he became head coach at Farragut, where he also taught algebra and geometry.

Nelson had Fields, the player Garnett had met at camp, who was already a marvelous player as a junior. Also on the team were sophomore Lakeith Henderson, and senior Garnett, now 6'11" tall. The 6'3" Fields, a great leaper, would be an All-State player by the end of the season. Going into his senior season, Fields, a guard, was rated as the fifth-best college prospect in the country by leading recruiting experts.

When the 1995-1996 high school basketball season began, Farragut played before packed houses. In early January, Farragut was ranked No. 2 in Illinois. Defending Class AA champion Peoria Manual was No. 1.

Already there was talk about whether Garnett would skip college and go straight to the NBA.

In mid-January, now No. 1-ranked Farragut played Rock Island, ranked No. 16 in the state. The *Chicago Tribune* reported, "This was the game everyone came to see." Fields and Garnett, known as KG, didn't disappoint the standing-room-only crowd of 5,400. The Farragut Admirals had too much athleticism for Rock Island. Fields put on a spectacular dunking exhibition as Farragut won, 69-57. Garnett himself had several crowd-pleasing slams while scoring 23 points and pulling down 19 rebounds.

USA Today would rank Farragut No. 3 in the nation during the season. The Admirals won the school's first public league championship and

Garnett reacts with obvious pride with under a minute left in the game against Carver for the 1995 Chicago Public League championship.

Towering over Thornton's players, Garnett takes a shot for the Farragut Admirals.

would finish the season with a 28-2 record. Garnett averaged 26 points and 18 rebounds per game. He also had seven assists and six blocked shots per game.

Only four times in the past 35 years had a Chicago school won an Illinois state high school boys basketball championship.

Farragut's attempt to win the Class AA Illinois state championship came to a startling finish on a mid-March 1995 night. The Admirals faced the underdog Thorton Wildcats in the state quarterfinals. The Thorton coach had a plan to stop All-American Garnett, but Coach Rocky Hill's players thought he was crazy.

"Man, Kevin Garnett is a great player," said Thorton guard Chauncey Jones. "Did I believe my coach at first? Not really. It was like, 'Man, come on. Nobody has stopped Kevin all year long.'"

Garnett had what would have been a good night for most high school players—17 points, 16 rebounds, six blocks, and three steals. But he had come into the game averaging 25 points and 18 rebounds a game. The difference was enough for Thorton, beaten only once in 30 games, to upset the Admirals, 46-43.

Under Coach Hill's game plan, Thorton switched between man-to-man and 1-3-1 zone defenses. Thorton's 6'9" sophomore center Melvin Ely played Garnett tight and when Garnett, who was 6'11", got the ball, Ely received defensive help from the strong-side (the side of the floor where the ball is) guard and wing. The weakside (the side away from the ball) guard collapsed into the lane to block an escape pass from Garnett to his 6'8" freshman teammate Michael Wright.

That meant four of five players were dealing with Farragut's two big men. Coach Hill acknowledged that left his best defender, Tai Streets, all alone to deal with Farragut's other star, Fields. Hill's team let Fields take wide-open shots from the free-throw circle and the top of the key. But the coach wanted Streets to stop Fields from driving the lane.

Ely and the other Wildcats leaned on Garnett, and Thorton led 29-20 at halftime despite Fields's 16 points. A Garnett basket with 50 seconds to play in the fourth quarter brought Farragut within one point, 44-43. Two free throws gave a three-point lead back to Farragut, and Garnett missed a three-point attempt that would have sent the game into overtime.

After the game, Ely said it had made him angry that Garnett was looking past Thorton to the next team. "In the newspaper," Ely said, "Garnett said he was looking forward to playing Peoria Manual. Man, all dogs got teeth, and they got bit."

Peoria Manual, meanwhile, went on to repeat as state champion.

MINNESOTA

4
THE BIG JUMP

Garnett's high school basketball days were over. He was one of the nation's most sought-after players, but there was a problem. His college test scores were below what was required by the National Collegiate Athletic Association to play basketball at an NCAA college. He would not be given a college scholarship, and he would have to sit out one year of college as a Proposition 48 athlete.

His other option was to declare himself eligible for early entry into the 1995 NBA draft.

Eight months later, Garnett would tell a Chicago sportswriter that "going pro was my second option." If he had been eligible, he said, he would have gone to Maryland or Michigan. A South Carolina newspaper reported before Garnett's final year of high school that he was favoring Michigan.

In April 1995, Garnett played in the 18th annual McDonald's All-American game with other

NBA Commissioner David Stern congratulates Kevin Garnett after the Minnesota Timberwolves drafted him out of high school.

Kevin and his high school coach, William Nelson, get ready to announce his decision to enter the NBA draft.

high school standouts from across the nation. He won the John Wooden Most Valuable Player Award, named for the legendary former UCLA coach, and received the award from Wooden himself after the game at Kiel Center in St. Louis. Interestingly, Wooden preferred basketball without frills and did not like the dunk shot, a sharp contrast to Garnett's flashy style.

A couple days later a Chicago paper said, "Sometime in the next month, Kevin Garnett will make the decision of a lifetime." The decision became evident when Garnett did not show up to take a college entrance test he had been scheduled to take. And in May, Garnett mailed a letter to the NBA making himself available for the 1995 draft on June 28 in Toronto. He beat the early-entry deadline by three days.

Orlando Magic player Nick Anderson, a former star at Simeon High School in Chicago and the University of Illinois, said Garnett was taking "a giant step."

Garnett would be only the fourth American-born player ever to skip college and go directly to the pros through the NBA draft. More would follow.

Later, Garnett said that he "always thought big" while he was growing up.

"You're never supposed to think small," he said. "You can reach something small in a heartbeat. But when you have big aspirations of yourself and you reach it, that's special."

Despite his youth, Garnett had shown he was not afraid to make hard choices. He made the move from South Carolina to Chicago, even though many teenagers his age wouldn't have wanted to change schools for their senior year.

In June, a dozen NBA general managers conducted a mock draft. They had Garnett going to the Minnesota Timberwolves as the fifth pick overall in the 1995 draft. They were right on target—that's exactly what happened when the Wolves made their first selection.

In October 1995, Garnett officially became a professional player when he signed a three-year contract with the Timberwolves. The contract was worth $5.6 million, the most it could be under the NBA's labor agreement with the players. The Wolves were prepared to build their franchise around the tall, thin teenager.

Flip Saunders and Kevin McHale knew right away they were getting someone special. They had gone to a Chicago gym in the spring of 1995 to watch the high school senior work out a couple weeks before the NBA draft.

Saunders, then the Timberwolves' general manager, has often told the following story.

Kevin Garnett and Timberwolves vice president Kevin McHale talk at a news conference after Garnett became part of the Minnesota Timberwolves.

"When we went in there to watch him work out, we thought we'd tell everyone we liked this kid, in the hopes that someone would take him. . . ." They hoped one of the other players in the 1995 draft would drop down to the fifth spot in time for the Wolves to make their choice.

Instead, Saunders broke into a sweat when he and his longtime friend and boss walked out of the gym. They both recognized Garnett was extremely skilled, a player they could really use—if they could draft him. Saunders looked at McHale and said, "We're telling nobody."

Saunders and McHale easily recognized Garnett's basketball talent. But they were gambling that he would have the character and personality to successfully make the huge leap from high school to the NBA. The Timberwolves needed that to happen. They were a six-year-old franchise when they drafted Garnett. The most games they had ever won was 29 in their second year.

They had lost at least 53 of their 82 games each year.

Saunders has said they didn't know if Garnett could make the big jump. But one thing impressed the Wolves' executives on their first meeting in the Chicago gym. After the workout, Garnett was sitting on the floor. "When we walked up to him," Saunders said, "he jumped up and said, 'Mr. McHale and Mr. Saunders.' When you talk to him, Kevin looks you right in the eye.

"I knew then, that kid is going to be like a sponge. You could see it in his eye, his focus, his concentration. He was going to absorb everything that we taught him."

The lessons began when the Timberwolves opened their training camp for the 1995-96 season on September 18, 1995. The focus was on the Timberwolves' man-child who had the size and basketball skills of a man, but who was still a teenager in an adult world. Observers said Garnett struggled at times on his first day of NBA practice.

A month later, Garnett and the Timberwolves were playing preseason exhibition games. Asked if he was excited to be an NBA player, Garnett answered, "I'm not excited, but I'm happy to have the opportunity to go out and work hard and try to do better."

During the 1995-1996 preseason, Garnett started three games and averaged 9.1 points a game during the exhibition games. When the regular season began, he would come off the bench and play the small forward position rather than center, as he had done in high school.

McHale had good things to say about Garnett after watching him in the preseason. A Minnesota native and former University of Minnesota star,

Kevin Garnett reaches for the ball in his first game in the NBA against the Sacramento Kings.

McHale had been an elite player during a long career as an All-Star forward with the Boston Celtics. Glen Taylor, the team's new owner, had put McHale in charge of the Timberwolves basketball operations in May 1995.

Garnett, McHale said, is "a player [who] helps get the final score in your favor."

Less than five months after graduating from Farragut Academy, Garnett was testing those instincts in a real NBA game. He came off the bench with 5:55 left in the first quarter of the November 3, 1995, Wolves season opener against the Sacramento Kings in California. Two minutes later, he maneuvered into the low post and took a pass from Wolves forward Tom Gugliotta. A bank shot produced his first NBA field goal.

Gaining confidence as he stayed on the floor in the second quarter, Garnett twice found teammate Marques Bragg open inside and threaded the ball to him for two field goals in a 7-0 Timberwolves run. Garnett would take only three more shots in the game, making all of them, contrasting with the Wolves' below par 36.7 field-goal shooting for the game. The poor shooting resulted in a 95-86 Kings victory. Garnett played 16 minutes in his professional debut and had one rebound and one assist to go along with his eight points.

Four days later he played in his first NBA victory, a 93-92 win over the Lakers in Minneapolis. On November 16, Garnett went into double figures for the first time as a pro, scoring 19 points as the Wolves lost at home to the San Antonio Spurs, 105-96.

Flip Saunders became the head coach of the Minnesota Timberwolves in December of 1995.

On December 18, 1995, with Garnett still coming off the bench for the Wolves, the team got a new coach. The Wolves fired Bill Blair and named general manager Saunders the new head coach. Saunders had won two championships while coaching in the Continental Basketball Association. He was a college teammate of Wolves vice president McHale at the University of Minnesota.

By this time, Garnett had decided he was happy with his brief pro experience. "Practice hard, recover, have the whole rest of the day to myself? If I can't enjoy this, I ought to get another life," he said.

Garnett, however, was learning how different it was to play in the NBA. Coaches got after him and made him work hard every day. He was also lugging around the team's ball bags, a rookie's chore. He said at the time that he would not recommend that other high school stars follow his lead. "There's nothing easy about the NBA," he said. Away from the basketball court, the Timber-

Garnett had a very successful rookie season and used his long arms to grab rebound after rebound.

wolves brass had not been sure how to deal with a 19-year-old. They had thought about finding a family in the Minneapolis area with whom he could live. They also thought about having a chaperone for him when the Wolves were on the road.

Early on, they decided that such steps would not be necessary. Garnett was used to being on his own and had been doing his own housekeeping, including the laundry, for a long time.

"I know what it is like to have nothing," he recalled. "You look at things much differently when you wash out your own socks at night and then wear them the next day. I'll never forget what those days were like or forget where I came from. But you know, I also know I'm never going back to those days either. I've come from having very little to living my dream."

Garnett's old Mauldin buddy, Jamie Peters—nicknamed "Bug"—had joined him in Minneapolis. "Bug, he's my best friend, my man, since I was four," Garnett said. "He's my man, my brother, my shadow, that's me."

After beginning his rookie season coming off the bench, Garnett started the Wolves' final 42 games. At season's end, he had averaged almost 29 minutes a game and played in all but two of the 82 regular season contests. The Timberwolves' record in Garnett's rookie season was 26-56. He averaged 10.4 points a game, making eight of the 28 three-point shots he took during the year. He had 6.3 rebounds and 1.6 blocks a game, and fouled out of only two games.

He tied the Timberwolves' rookie record with 19 rebounds against Philadelphia late in the season. Earlier, he had scored eight points in the Schick Rookie Game during the 1996 NBA All-Star weekend in San Antonio, Texas.

A year later, deep into his second pro season, Garnett told a magazine writer, "I love my life." Mike Lupica wrote, ". . . it turned out that Garnett could handle himself with the older boys. The kid turned out to be a good kid." Garnett, Lupica pointed out, was polite.

Garnett guards Damon Stoudamire in the NBA Rookie Game during his first All-Star weekend.

The Timberwolves were a much improved team in 1996-97. The team reached two milestones during the season. They won 40 games, the most ever in their eight-year history. When the Wolves beat the Clippers, 108-96, in Los Angeles on April 10, 1997, they gained a second milestone. The win put them in the NBA playoffs for the very first time. The Wolves were no longer the laughing stock of the NBA.

The win over the Clippers earned the Wolves the sixth playoff position in the NBA's Western Conference. However, their appearance in the playoffs was brief. The Houston Rockets set an NBA playoff record for most three-point shots made and for most attempted in a three-game series as they swept the Wolves 3-0 in the first-round series. Garnett averaged 17.3 points a game in his first NBA playoff action.

21

5

BIG MONEY AND A WINNING RECORD

The focus on Garnett grew more intense when he signed the largest contract in the history of professional sports on October 1, 1997. The Timberwolves signed a contract extension paying him $126 million. The six-year deal on average would pay him $21 million a year—more than $256,000 per game for the 82-game regular season.

In actuality, the money would not be evenly distributed over the six years. For example, Garnett was expected to make $14 million in the 1998-99 season, the first year of the new contract.

The deal with Garnett is worth almost $40 million more than what Taylor, the Timberwolves' owner, paid for the team in 1995, $88.5 million.

Vice president McHale said the Timberwolves signed Garnett to a deal that would clearly define him as a future superstar. The new contract

Garnett dunks the ball, showing the agility and ability that helped him land a record-breaking NBA contract.

Garnett gives an interview after signing a history-making six-year contract.

demonstrated McHale's growing confidence in Garnett.

The Wolves entered the season with two other high-profile players, second-year point guard Stephon Marbury and veteran power forward Tom Gugliotta.

A third of the way through the season, Garnett had his first triple-double—earning double figures in three statistical categories. He had 18 points, 13 rebounds, and 10 assists against the Denver Nuggets at the Target Center in downtown Minneapolis on January 3, 1998. It was only one of 12 triple-doubles recorded in the NBA that season.

Garnett downplayed the triple-double and was

more satisfied with the Wolves victory. However, the triple-double showed that Garnett could do more than just score. Wolves coach Saunders said Garnett "is a guy [who] is always going to be a double-double guy, and he's always going to be on that edge of getting the assists."

A few weeks later, Garnett, midway through his third year as a pro, seemed to be hit hard by some of the realities of life. Maybe he was discovering that work is work and not always fun, even if work is playing basketball. Perhaps it was the stress that can come from stardom.

At any rate, Garnett told a Minneapolis reporter who covers the Timberwolves that he wasn't enjoying himself as much as he had in his first two seasons.

"It's about me just enjoying the game," he told the *Star Tribune*'s Steve Aschburner. "My boys always tell me when I come off the floor, 'What's wrong? It's like you got something on your mind.' Sometimes I don't have an answer for 'em. The other 20,000 [fans] who watch us can see it.

"Sometimes, I feel like Steph [Marbury] is doing my job of pumping up the crowd. . . . I don't think I've raised the roof in this building once this year. I don't know, I think I'm acting like my mom instead of KG, two one [21 is Garnett's Timberwolves uniform number]."

It was important Garnett enjoy himself—for the future of the team. More than a year earlier, Aschburner foresaw Garnett as ". . . at once, the Wolves present and future, the player around whom the franchise designs ticket campaigns and isolation plays."

Garnett's upbeat personality and positive attitude soon returned. Once again, he was joking with players, team employees, and reporters.

Reaching over the head of Miami Heat forward Billy Owens, Garnett grabs for the ball.

Then, in February 1998, fans voted Garnett onto the starting five of the Western Conference team in the annual NBA All-Star Game. The February 8 game at Madison Square Garden was Garnett's second consecutive All-Star Game.

He had been added to the Western Conference team for the 1997 game as a replacement player. The league named him as one of two injury replacements. At 20, he was the second-youngest All-Star in league history. He scored 10 points in the game. Garnett was on his way to being a top level NBA player.

It was not surprising to McHale, who had watched Garnett's growth as a pro player.

"From a purist standpoint, he does all the little things very well," McHale said. "From a spectacular standpoint, he makes about two or three plays a game that are astonishing, really eye-catching stuff."

Rod Thorn, NBA vice president of operations, said, "The vast majority of players coming out of high school aren't physically and mentally ready for the challenge of our league." But Garnett and the Los Angeles Lakers' Kobe Bryant were, Thorn said.

"Few players coming out of high school can acclimate themselves as well as Kevin and Kobe have," Thorn said.

Minnesota closed the 1997-98 season on a run, winning 12 of their final 16 games. They had done so without forward Tom Gugliotta and guard Chris Carr. The 6'10", 240-pound Gugliotta was a starting forward before he underwent season-ending knee surgery March 3 and missed the final 39 games. Gugliotta, 28, was in his sixth pro season and was the team's leading scorer when he went down. Also missing from the Wolves playoff roster was the 6'6" Carr, with a severe ankle sprain. Carr missed the final 19 games of the season after starting 40 of the first 42 games.

One of the late season games was at the Los Angeles Sports Arena. A win over the hometown Clippers would cinch a playoff berth for the second straight season. Garnett batted away Rodney Rogers' shot in the lane with nine seconds to play during the Clippers' chance to tie the game. This saved the win and meant there would be a postseason for the Timberwolves. Garnett had 17 points and seven assists in the March 27, 1998, 100-98 victory.

Some say the mark of a superstar is how well his team does. When the 1997-98 regular season ended on April 19, 1998, the Timberwolves had a winning record, 45-37, for the first time in their nine-year history and finished third in the Midwest division. Garnett was sending a message to the league that he was going to be a top talent.

TIMBERWOLVES
21

6

"A Pack of Wolves"

The Wolves had the seventh playoff slot in the Western Conference, putting them against the Seattle SuperSonics in first round play. *USA Today* said the Timberwolves' chances of winning the NBA title were 750-1.

The Sonics were known for their ball-hawking, trapping defense. Led by their quick, aggressive 6'4" All-Star point guard Gary Payton, Seattle continually tried to pressure the player with the ball. Payton was perhaps the best one-on-one defender in the league. The Sonics defense concentrated on forcing turnovers and converting them into baskets. Seattle ranked fourth in the NBA during the 1997-98 season in producing turnovers.

Another goal of the Sonics' defense was to keep the ball away from the opponent's best player. To accomplish what they wanted, the Sonics always tried to bring a second defender to the man with the ball, and they switched without

Kevin Garnett maneuvers around Seattle SuperSonics forward Jerome Kersey in the 1998 NBA playoffs.

Garnett shoots over the head of Seattle SuperSonic Detlef Schrempf to score for the Timberwolves' playoff hopes.

hesitation. They didn't care if Payton ended up guarding a seven-footer. Wolves coach Saunders said the way Seattle played was "very much a controlled chaos."

The Timberwolves had four days to practice before the first playoff game in Seattle's Key Arena on April 24. They watched Seattle game film and practiced against the constant pressure all over the floor.

Seattle wanted to force the ballhandler to pass the ball by sending a second defender at him. Coach Saunders's solution was to have Wolves players play off the ball, make their moves away from the man with the ball. A player off the ball would not have defensive pressure. He could catch a pass and shoot it. The message was: "If you don't do those two things, you have no chance at all," the coach said.

As the Timberwolves practiced at Key Arena the morning of the playoff opener, Garnett expressed confidence in himself and his team, despite doubts by some observers. Marbury thought he was ready to handle Seattle's pressure.

The Timberwolves thought they could compete with Seattle even though they'd lost 26 games to the Sonics—an NBA record—before winning in Seattle, 112-103, on December 23, 1997. Overall, they had lost 29 of the last 30 games they'd played against Seattle.

When the first game got underway, the Sonics scored the game's first eight points. The Wolves trailed 12-2 before the game was three minutes old.

Minnesota did not make their jump shots or any other kind, either. They made only 31 of 92 shots for 33.7 percent from the field. Wolves shooting guard Anthony Peeler missed his first 12 shots and was 3 for 18 for the game including zero for six from three-point range.

Seattle forward Vin Baker scored 14 points in the first quarter on the way to a game-high 25 points as the Sonics waltzed to a 108-83 victory. Garnett led the Wolves in scoring with 18 from the field and his 18 rebounds led both teams.

The Timberwolves were embarrassed by the game, and Saunders said, "You want to crawl into a hole after a game like that." The coach said his team had to be "more aggressive" and "create more energy" in Game 2.

Saunders decided to go to a small lineup for Game 2. It was a lineup he had used with some success at times late in the regular season. He started three guards, the 6'2" Marbury, mid-season acquisition Peeler, who was 6'4", and 6'3" Terry Porter, who was in his 13th NBA season and had been coming off the bench. Garnett was the center, and the other starter was 6'7" Sam Mitchell.

When Saunders told Marbury he planned to go small, the young point guard said he looked at his coach as if he were crazy. "I said to myself,

'We're gonna get killed in the paint,'" Marbury said.

Minnesota played "like a pack of wolves," as Saunders put it, pestering the Sonics into 14 turnovers and leading for most of the game on the way to their first-ever playoff victory. The small guys did not get murdered in the paint. They out-rebounded the home team 49-37 in the 98-93 victory on April 26.

Four of the five starters were in double figures, led by Marbury's 25. Peeler still had trouble shooting, going 4 for 14 and zero for two from long range. Astonishingly, however, he had a game-high 14 rebounds, six more than Garnett, who scored 15 points. Garnett got into serious foul trouble early and played only 32 minutes, well below his series average of 39 minutes. Even so, Garnett got the go-ahead goal.

Even with the fouls, Garnett said, "I knew I had to be more aggressive, yet cautious. When I saw open spots, I tried to take advantage of them. And when I saw loose balls, I tried to get them up as quick as possible."

Surely the veteran SuperSonics would establish their superiority when the series moved back to Minneapolis for Game 3. Before the April 28th game, the Wolves were still underdogs. Seattle was again favored to win, but this time they were favored by only six points.

But this was the game when Garnett asserted himself in the fourth quarter and led Minnesota to the 98-90 victory. Mitchell had a playoff career high 19 points in the game. The Timberwolves had done what probably nobody thought they could do, take a two-to-one series lead in the NBA playoffs.

Nobody maybe except the Timberwolves themselves. They believed they could win. "If you don't believe it, you find ways that you can lose," said Saunders.

Sonics reserve guard Nate McMillan said the Wolves "small ball" lineup was hurting his team. Seattle had depended on their aggressive defense,

Minnesota's Anthony Peeler, right, encourages his teammate during the 1998 NBA playoffs.

and Minnesota's small, quick lineup had overcome that advantage.

The Wolves, however, then lost a golden opportunity to win their first playoff series ever despite team high points (20) and rebounds (10) from Garnett. A 10-2 Seattle run gave the Sonics a 77-67 lead with 8:37 to play in the April 30th game. The Timberwolves never got back into it. Payton and Hawkins both scored 24 points for Seattle, and Hawkins smothered the Wolves' Marbury, who made only 4 of 16 field goal attempts and had five turnovers.

The 92-88 loss, their first at home in eight games, forced the Timberwolves to return to Seattle for a winner-take-all game. "It's going to be hard, as hard as it was tonight [Game 4]," Coach Saunders said. "It's something we can do, because we've won two of the last three times we've played [in Key Arena], so it's not that uncomfortable."

Reporter Aschburner wrote on May 2, the day of the deciding game, that ". . . Seattle still has a healthier, deeper, more talented roster than the Wolves." He was correct.

Playing before a full house of 17,072 home fans on a Saturday afternoon, Seattle outscored Minnesota by 16 points in the second half to win 97-84 and end the Timberwolves season. "We ran out of gas," Saunders said.

Seattle had concentrated its defense on the Wolves' two young stars. It had worked. Garnett and Marbury had only seven points apiece even though both played just about the entire 48-minute game. Garnett also had turned over the ball 10 times, the most turnovers in his pro career.

Garnett, who did not score in the second half,

was lined up next to Sonics forward Detlef Schrempf awaiting a free throw near the game's end. "I didn't have it tonight," he told Schrempf. "You guys really brought it to us."

Schrempf, playing in his 13th NBA season, smiled. "You've got about 21 more of these [playoffs] in your future," he told the anguished Garnett. "I've got maybe two or less."

The Timberwolves went home and the Sonics went on to a second-round series against a Pacific-Division rival, the Los Angeles Lakers, who steamrolled the Sonics in four straight games after Los Angeles lost Game 1.

21

7

"I Want the Sky"

The Timberwolves now looked forward to the 1998-99 season. Garnett would head to the weight room during the summer of 1998 to add strength. "He has to do what Scottie Pippen did, get in the weight room and get a lot stronger," said Coach Saunders, "so people can't push him around."

In the 1998-99 season, Garnett would be paid under his new contract and expectations were higher. The Timberwolves believed Garnett had the talent and the work ethic necessary to reach those expectations. Garnett brought quick feet, good hands, and leaping ability to the court, along with his height. These attributes help make him a complete player.

Garnett is one of the hard workers. He works as hard or harder on the defensive end of the floor as he does when the Wolves have the ball. He is viewed by the Wolves' coaching staff as a

Kevin Garnett chases the ball and his dream of NBA stardom.

Garnett scores past the defense of Sacramento King Corliss Williamson.

dedicated, even ferocious defensive player. "It hurts me when someone scores on me," he says.

With his height and reach, he challenges opponents' shots. He is the Wolves' best shot-swatter. He has the foot speed and agility to guard a much smaller player if he picks one up on a switch.

"He plays outstanding defense," says Coach Saunders. He was concerned at the beginning that "we were going to have to spend most of our time explaining defensive concepts. I was amazed. He walked in knowing those things.

"Basically, Kevin has a photographic memory. He can recall how he guarded people two years ago, what they did against him, what he can do now to counter that."

"I want to be known as a great defensive player," Garnett said. "I take a lot of pride in my defense. I'd rather have 10 points and my guy have five, than for me to have 30 points and he has 30 points."

Garnett was one of only four NBA players with both 100 or more steals (he had 139) and 100 or more blocked shots (he had 150) in 1997-98. He set the team record for blocks in a season with 164 the previous year.

Since he carries only 220 pounds on his long

frame, Garnett can get pushed out of position when he posts up low. Stronger opponents, such as the Lakers 7'1", 315-pound Shaquille O'Neal, can push him several feet away from the basket.

Though he has improved his rebounding totals each year, Garnett does not bang on the boards with the best of the NBA's behemoths. A stronger Garnett is expected to be a better rebounder. TNT television commentator Doc Rivers, once an NBA player, has said Garnett improves every time he takes to the floor. Rivers said Garnett's success isn't related just to his athletic talent. Rivers said "it's more than that. This kid has style. He's got that [Seattle Mariners baseball star] Ken Griffey Jr. charisma. That's something nobody else can teach him. You're either born with it, or you're not. And Kevin Garnett was born with it."

"Kevin's personality does a lot for him," says teammate and friend Marbury. "And the league sees that. The NBA can build who they want to be for their stars, but it's not like they're building somebody who can't play. Kevin just has the personality to go with it."

Garnett is now 22 and has played three seasons with the Timberwolves. The questions about his choice to go from high school to the NBA have been answered. Not only can he play in the NBA, he is headed for NBA stardom.

Houston Rockets star forward Charles Barkley is a 14-year NBA veteran and not one who often praises young players. He said Garnett "can be as good as he wants to be."

During the 1998 first round playoff series with Seattle, Sonics coach George Karl said he thought

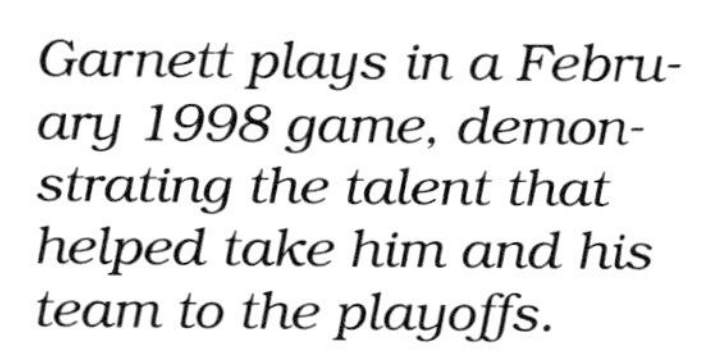
Garnett plays in a February 1998 game, demonstrating the talent that helped take him and his team to the playoffs.

Garnett "is earning his money. He's doing a very nice job."

Wolves teammate Gugliotta says Garnett "has a lot of room to grow. He plays well now, but after four, five, six years, when his body matures, he's going to be a whole 'nother kind of player."

Reporter Aschburner said in 1998 that "Kevin

Garnett, even at 18, even on the brink of what seemed like a reckless and arrogant decision, had the physical talent and potential to thrive in the NBA straight out of high school. No one, though, could have guessed the skinny kid from South Carolina, by way of Chicago's Ashland Avenue, had the head and the heart to make it happen so fast."

Garnett, himself, says, "I want the sky, and I'm not going to stop until I reach the top."

Chronology

1976	Born in Mauldin, South Carolina, on May 19, 1976
Late 1980s	Hones his game playing on the outdoor courts in Springfield Park, his love for the game catching the attention of Mauldin residents
1991	As 6'6" ninth grader, starts in high school team's first game of season
1994	In his senior year of high school, moves from South Carolina to play basketball in Chicago
1995	Just days after finishing high school, chosen fifth in the 1995 NBA draft, the first pick of the Minnesota Timberwolves
1997	On October 1, signs the largest contract in the history of professional sports—$126 million for six years
1998	On January 3 has his first triple-double—double figures in three statistical categories—in an NBA game with 18 points, 13 rebounds, and 10 assists against the Denver Nuggets; after Timberwolves finish season with most wins ever, he scores 15 points in a 98-93 victory over the Seattle SuperSonics on April 26 for the Timberwolves' first playoff victory in their history

STATISTICS

NBA Regular Season

Year	G	FGM	FGA	PTS	PPG	RPG	BLK	AST	APG	STL
1995-96	80	361	735	835	10.4	6.3	131	145	1.8	86
1996-97	77	549	1,100	1,309	17.0	8.0	163	236	3.1	105
1997-98	82	635	1,293	1,518	18.5	9.6	150	348	4.2	139
Career	239	1,545	3,128	3,662	15.3	8.0	444	729	3.1	330

G games
FGM field goals made
FGA field goals attempted
PTS points
PPG points per game
RPG rebounds per game
BLK blocks
AST assists
APG assists per game
STL steals

FURTHER READING

Aschburner, Steve. "Wild Ride Reaches Exit." *Minneapolis Star Tribune*, May 3, 1998.

Aschburner, Steve. "An Acquired Distaste." *Minneapolis Star Tribune,* April 24, 1998.

Barreiro, Dan. "It All Comes Around." *Minneapolis Star Tribune,* April 24, 1998.

McCallum, Jack. "Hoop Dream." *Sports Illustrated.* June 26, 1995.

Smith, Sam. "'Kid' Garnett Takes on Man-Sized Job." *Chicago Tribune*, November 2, 1995.

Tuttle, Dennis. *The Composite Guide to Basketball.* Philadelphia: Chelsea House Publishers, 1998.

Vancil, Mark. *NBA Basketball Basics.* New York: Sterling Publishing Company, 1995.

About the Author

Paul J. Deegan has written some 80 books, including titles on the United States Supreme Court, American universities, and the nations of the Persian Gulf. Subjects of the many biographies he's written include presidents and athletes.

Paul is a graduate of the University of Minnesota. A former newspaper editor, he has worked for years in publishing as an editor and administrator.

Paul and his wife, Dorothy, have three adult children and five grandchildren. They reside in Eden Prairie, Minnesota, a suburb of Minneapolis.

PHOTO CREDITS
AP/Wide World Photos: pp. 2, 8, 10, 13, 16, 19, 22, 30, 32, 34, 36, 37, 38, 39, 40, 42, 44, 46, 48, 51, 54, 56, 58; *Chicago Sun-Times*: p. 26, ©1996, reprinted with permission; *Chicago Tribune*: pp. 24, 27, 28, photos by Jose Osorio and Ed Wagner.

INDEX

BROADVIEW PUBLIC LIBRARY DISTRICT
2226 S. 16th AVENUE
BROADVIEW, IL 60153
(708) 345-1325